Melinda Fouts

# Cognitive Enlightenment

## A Disciplining of Your Mind

novum ◢◤ premium

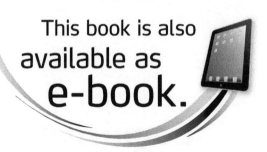

This book is also available as e-book.

www.novumpublishing.com

© 2019 novum publishing

ISBN 978-1-64268-088-1
Editing: Karen Simmering
Cover photo:
Pop Nukoonrat | Dreamstime.com
Cover design, layout & typesetting:
novum publishing

**www.novumpublishing.com**

# Contents

# Synopsis

## to Cognitive Enlightenment

Cognitive enlightenment is a process of delving deep into the self to gain greater understanding of how one disrupts one's own inner peace. Mastering cognitive enlightenment is a daily discipline of watching one's thoughts and how emotions are stirred up that one can control and transcend.

In this book, I take the reader through ways to begin mastering and owning their thoughts from my 20-plus years in private practice as a psychotherapist. The first six chapters are devoted to the areas where we need to put ourselves under a microscope to begin this journey. The last two chapters are stories about an individual whose experience amplifies many points I address and my struggle with attaining cognitive enlightenment. It is my hope that through these two stories individuals will understand the importance and the challenge it is to attain cognitive enlightenment yet at the same time, be encouraged to start the journey.

Melinda Fouts, Ph.D.
309 Paseo Rd.
Carbondale, CO 81623
970-274-3130
melinda@successstartswithyou.net

*My journey through life brought
many teachers even though they
did not hold the title of teacher.
I dedicate this book to all the
teachers I have met along my path
and most especially to my daughter,
Serena. I also dedicate this book
to my granddaughter, Seleste Elliette,
may you be a peace maker on your journey
through this life.*

# Introduction

The inspiration for this book grew out of over 20 years' experience as a professional in the business of being a shrewd observer of human behavior. Actually, my observation began at the young and impressionable age of five when my father would take me on trips to attend business and political meetings with him. He did not bring along crayons and paper for me; rather, he insisted that I sit and pay attention. And I did.

Since no one paid attention to me during these meetings, it allowed me to observe and take in everything: their faces, their body language, the tone of the speaker and the emotional climate of the room. I listened and studied the whole of the individual. I observed what wasn't spoken, the body language expressed in the face, eyes, arms, and even the slightest shift in attitude. I could tell through the eyes, mood, and facial expression, ever so slight, whether someone agreed, disagreed, was becoming irritated, wasn't listening and so on.

Over time, I learned that people are not very good listeners in general. They are formulating their thoughts and responses, not fully taking in the information from whomever is speaking. Their minds have been shaped over time, including what they think and believe, and their response is a result of their perspectives and beliefs. Even their decisions are driven by their beliefs, by the thoughts they keep telling themselves, by their storyline and their culture, all that shaped them to be who they are today.

As a professional with a private practice for over 20 years as a psychotherapist and an executive coach, I honed my skills and craft discovering further what keeps individuals stuck. When repetitive beliefs and perspectives are reinforced, one stays stuck in one's box, and this is how one gets in the way of one's own success, whether it is an observable success or an inner sense driven by fear that one is truly not successful. Everyone's individual box is ripe for creating unnecessary conflict and undue suffering both for the individual and those around them.

For more than half my life, I have exercised a daily mindfulness practice that has brought awareness to how our thoughts and mind chatter can create patterns of behavior that are difficult to break. With this daily practice, I became aware of the negative self-talk that plays and undermines confidence, being and feeling successful and having an inner peace. We all have that negative tape hidden deep down and may not even know the root message. For the majority of my clients, the root of the tape is feeling "not good enough" or "not worthy." To get out of this trap, one needs to adopt a mindfulness practice to start having greater self-awareness. From this daily practice, you become more cognitive of what your thoughts are and then can make a choice to change the tape and quiet the mental chatter as these thoughts are limiting our fullest potential.

Throughout my life and career, having a mindfulness practice is paramount to achieve cognitive enlightenment and transcend our limiting thought processes. It is the gateway to disciplining the mind. In this book, we will explore re-engineering the landscape of your self-image from the identities you have created for yourself, your projections, your limiting thoughts, and so much more. It will be taking mindfulness to the next level.

Wanting to reach more people, I decided it was time to share what I have observed and learned throughout my life and how we can untether ourselves from our thought patterns. This book is for anyone who wants inner peace by discovering what landmines your own thoughts create in your life. It is not a self-help book. Rather, it is a book to invite you and entice you to self-discovery. My dream and mission is if you can arrive at inner peace we will be one step closer to world peace. It is up to each of us to take charge of our thoughts, words, and actions, moving the globe toward one of peaceful cognitive enlightenment.

The first six chapters are an exploration of what keeps us from inner peace and attaining cognitive enlightenment. The last two chapters are stories about attaining cognitive enlightenment.

# Chapter One

## What Is Cognitive Enlightenment?

When we consider cognitive enlightenment, we need to fully understand the two terms before we can marry them together. Here is the definition of cognition according to Wikipedia:

*Cognition is "the mental action or process of acquiring knowledge and understanding through thought, experience, and the senses." It encompasses processes such as attention, the formation of knowledge, memory and working memory, judgment and evaluation, reasoning and "computation," problem solving and decision making, comprehension and production of language. Cognitive processes use existing knowledge and generate new knowledge.*

Breaking down this definition, the formation of knowledge is not without its biases because we formulate and evaluate that knowledge from our past experiences. Understanding that information is shaped by our pre-existing beliefs, our limiting beliefs and our culture. From the experience, we form judgments and evaluate the experience from our pre-existing conditioning. There are usually two categories of evaluating an experience: it is either a good experience or a bad experience, positive or negative. As we are driven by either pain or pleasure, we tend to limit ourselves so that we can stay comfortable and feel good.

One of the ways we do that is by staying in the realm of our comfort zone, areas that are familiar and confirm our beliefs, rather than, as the end of the definition states, generate new knowledge.

Let me give you an example of how we are shaped and limited from an early age. When my daughter was four years old, every morning I drove her to daycare. On a week where the full moon was lowering in the morning sky, each morning it was less and less full. By the third or fourth day, my daughter exclaimed, "Mommy, I don't think the moon should be up when the sun is up. It's melting!"

I chuckled and told her I agreed with her. I could have chosen a different response and explained the science behind what she was observing, but I knew that all too soon she would acquire that knowledge.

My point here is that I wanted her to continue to observe and state her observations without any interference from me. Often, when young children are told that they are incorrect, it squelches their curiosity. Being curious is the root of having an open mind and being able to absorb new knowledge that is out of our realm of tradition, beliefs, and perspectives, can take us out of our comfort zone and feeling numbly good.

By choosing to stay in our comfort zone, we are in the realm of what Daniel Kahneman, in his book, *Thinking, Fast and Slow*, refers to as cognitive ease. He explores how we are all subject to cognitive ease and abhor cognitive strain.

Cognitive ease makes us feel good and keeps us comfortably numb. When we use the knowledge that has been funneled into our comfort zone, we then take the position that how we interpreted the information is true and correct. From this stance, we assure ourselves and deepen our beliefs by thinking we are right and when we think we are right we become certain that we are right and experience a sense of feeling good, remaining in cognitive ease.

Being in a state of cognitive ease makes us feel good and our tendency is to believe what validates our pre-existing beliefs, making us comfortably unaware we are reinforcing our biases and beliefs. We also tend to buy in to what is familiar, often associated with our beliefs or what we have been exposed to over time, referred to as the mere-exposure effect. Finally, as implied by the term 'cognitive ease', we are more likely to believe what is easy. When it is familiar we are comfortable and therefore know it to be true and right. We all enjoy the feeling of being right! Right?

Cognitive strain is where we are in unfamiliar territory and have to apply ourselves. Think about when you first learned to tie your shoes. You had to concentrate hard and think through each step to accomplish the task. This makes us uncomfortable.

However, with time, tying your shoes became so easy and familiar that you can now tie your shoes, hold a conversation and think about your grocery list for dinner all at the same time. You moved from cognitive strain to cognitive ease.

What is important is that when it comes to cognitive enlightenment, we need to become comfortable with cognitive strain, which requires slowing down, paying attention to what you are thinking, your judgments, your beliefs, your biases, and finally what is called the negative bias.

Our brains are wired to be aware of anything that threatens our survival. Because of this wiring, we notice negative events more than we notice positive ones. Negative bias keeps us constantly evaluating experience and other people through the periscope of judgment mentioned earlier – either it is a good, positive experience or a bad, negative experience.

For example, generally, we experience difference as a threat. It puts us on alert, pulling us out of being comfortably numb. Negative bias is the driver behind the fears we have, whether warranted or not.

Part of the problem today is all the news media is negative amplifying fear in our culture. Moving toward cognitive enlightenment requires stepping away from the onslaught of negative news, so that you can move from a fear-based, negative thought process, which is like hitting the reset button on your computer for your brain.

Stemming from the work of Daniel Kahneman and his concepts of cognitive ease and cognitive strain, I want to take his idea a step further and challenge my readers to go beyond cognitive strain into cognitive enlightenment. Now that we have explored the meaning of cognitive, let's look at the definition of enlightenment.

There are several meanings of enlightenment. In the West, there was the age of enlightenment, a *"European intellectual movement of the late 17th and 18th centuries emphasizing reason and individualism rather than tradition. It was heavily influenced by 17th-century philosophers such as Descartes, Locke, and Newton, and its prominent figures included Kant, Goethe, Voltaire, Rousseau, and Adam Smith."* (From the Oxford online dictionary).

During this time, traditional beliefs, myths, and superstitions were being questioned and challenged, a necessary step for opening the mind to use reason and think outside the proverbial box. Examining and challenging cultural and personal beliefs was the bulk of the work of these 17th century philosophers. Their work was instrumental and important to the inner growth of individuals as a whole and society.

In addition to the age of enlightenment, there are the spiritual definitions to consider. There are several Asian words that are similar in meaning yet do not mean the same thing. However, the West has chosen enlightenment as the go-to translation for these different words.

For the purposes of this book, we will consider the definition of *Bodhi,* a Sanskrit word that means "awakening," and a perfection of insight into the Four Noble Truths. With this form of enlightenment, one ends all forms of personal stress, dissatisfaction, and suffering. I have chosen this definition because it comes closest to the purpose of this book.

Now that I have defined the two words, I can now assign a definition and have a better understanding of cognitive enlightenment. The definition I have created for Cognitive enlightenment is:

*"the process of paying attention to our mental thought processes, recognizing thought patterns that are driven by perspectives and beliefs, having awareness of our biases and awakening to and being open to choosing and navigating our thinking to be unattached to our ways of perceiving and transcend ourselves to utilize emotional and spiritual insight to create a higher and untethered thought process to bring about inner peace."*

Having awareness of what you are choosing to think at any moment and awareness of any visceral reaction to that thought is the process of cognition of your thought patterns and then perfecting your insight to a higher perspective outside of your limited perspective.

Years ago, I went to a lecture given by the Dalai Lama in Aspen, Colorado. At the end of his lecture, there was time for questions. A woman in the audience asked the Dalai Lama if he hated the Chinese for exiling him out of his country.

Her question caught my attention and I was anxious to hear his answer as I thought to myself, "He's the Dalai Lama, he is above hatred." I thought he was going to lecture us on the need to transcend hatred. I share my inner experience as this is how we can start paying attention to our visceral reactions, our perceptions and how belief is the driver behind it all.

His answer changed my life. When he heard the translated question, he smiled, then laughed. He nodded his head and said, "Yes, the Chinese have exiled me out of my country. Yes, they have burned sacred texts and sacred temples." Then pointing to his heart, he added, "Why would I let them in here, as I would be their prisoner?" Still pointing to his heart, he said, "Why would I give them the power to disrupt my inner peace?"

From that day forward, I became aware of how I let everything out of my power disrupt my inner peace, from situations to people.

Thus began my own journey toward cognitive enlightenment. It is a difficult journey and a road not well traveled but very much needed to change ourselves, thus changing the world. I believe if I can help one person find more inner peace then we are a step closer to world peace.

# Chapter Two

## Watching Your Thoughts, Mental Training

The other day, I was describing the essence of this book to a friend. I explained to her that to be cognitive of our thoughts we need to start paying attention to what we are thinking and feeling, developing a form of mental training by objectively watching our thoughts.

She asked a poignant question, "How do you watch your thoughts?" Pondering how best to answer her, I came up with this example.

Imagine that you are sitting in your seat on an airplane watching the other passengers walk down the aisle to their seats. As you look at each face, taking in their appearance, what are the thoughts running through your head about each person? Are you passing a quick judgment? What feelings are being stirred up? What reactions do you have toward each person?

From this example, you move from mindless mental chatter to mindful awareness of your thoughts, feelings, and even your prejudices and projections. You also become aware of how quickly your thoughts come and go. You are constantly making judgments and decisions, and Daniel Kahneman, (2016) in *Thinking, Fast and Slow*, writes:

*Judgments and decisions are guided directly by feelings of liking and disliking, with little deliberation or reasoning. Watching your thoughts brings into focus these random judgments and decisions allowing you to take control and manage them.*

Generally, during waking states, an abundance of mental activity is going on in our minds. This inner dialogue is constantly judging or criticizing, planning, and commenting, and it's all done by what we can refer to as a committee.

We all have this committee, which is continually talking inside our heads and from this continual chatter, emotions emerge, emotions that are toxic and create an unhealthy state of mind where we are not being conscious of our innermost selves. The Dalai Lama wrote:

*Nothing in the world can bother you as much as your own mind, I tell you. In fact, others seem to be bothering you, but it is not others. It is your own mind.*

His words emphasize the need for cognitive enlightenment as it is the way to bring peace to your mind. Watching your thoughts can also be approached by being aware of the emotions bubbling up inside of you; it is irrelevant whether it is the thoughts that capture your attention or the emotion. What is important is that you start paying attention to the turbulent, uncontrolled thoughts and emotions that create negative energy within you and in your environment.

In my article, *Increasing Emotional Intelligence Through Observing Thought-Waves,* published on LinkedIn 10/16/15, I presented an additional practice and steps to take for watching your thoughts through the analogy of watching waves at the ocean. Your thoughts can be overwhelming and powerful and when caught up in them, you can feel powerless. I wrote:

Our emotions, and our ingrained patterns can be like the various waves we encounter at the waters' edge. A thought-wave, (as I have decided to call it) can be so fierce that, once caught up in it, we are powerless to its hold. Just like waves, our thought-waves roll over our best intentions and our old reactions, our old patterns of responding take over, preventing us from achieving and being the way we want to respond under stress, under conflict, or those situations where miscommunications and misunderstandings have prevailed.

How then, do we push past these thought-waves? While the answer may sound simple, it is difficult and an ongoing process. The first step is to increase your self-awareness. Again, the answer provokes the question, HOW? How is this achieved? Below are some guidelines to start this journey:

1. Observance of the thought-waves and how they permeate your actions, decisions, and responses.

2. While observing, gain a removed perspective rather than getting caught up in the moment. Once caught up, the wave has taken control and you are no longer in control.

3. Heighten your senses, identifying what triggers the unwanted responses and ingrained behaviors that occur. Become intimately aware of your thought-waves and respect their power while knowing you can take control and respond differently.

4. Don't turn your back on these repetitive thought waves and pretend they will just go away. When we heighten our awareness and take ownership, we gain greater awareness in the moment as it is happening, and can alter our course.

5. Don't feel defeated.

It is worth repeating, "Don't feel defeated." Change is change and with a skilled leadership coach who specializes in this process, it takes time. I have a saying: If you have the awareness and the intention to change, it will happen. One more thought.

Some days at the beach, the waves are too big, too powerful to try and push through and go for a swim. At these times, it is best to sit on the beach and observe, watch their patterns and unrelenting persistence. Like some thought-waves, we need to be aware of what might be too big to take on by ourselves, and let go of trying to push through, knowing we could drown. At these times, it is best to sit and observe, and not get caught up in the power play.

Eventually, these waters that we were unable to navigate will subside into something more manageable. Once that has happened, it is time to push through and continue the path of expanding self-awareness through the intimate knowledge of your thought-waves.

Slowing down to become aware and analyze your thoughts is the process of watching your thoughts. It is like waking up to a clear, bluebird day after several days of fog, where you stop and breathe in the day, noting the brilliance of the sky. Slowing down and being aware of your surroundings makes you more conscious and observant.

Watching your thoughts is similar. You move into a more conscious state, allowing you to not only be aware of them, but you also can take control of your thoughts and emotions and choose those that are healthier, rather than being unconscious of the mental chatter. James Hillman described this type of awareness and the opposite stating:

*The primary qualifier of consciousness becomes participatory awareness – already indicated by the prefix con (with) ... Unconsciousness, rather than defined as unreflected (sic), means isolate, anaesthetized, unresponsive.* Archetypal Psychology, p. 71

From this description, Hillman amplifies the issue of becoming a participant with consciousness. The antithesis, as he points out in his definition of unconsciousness, is that you are not only unaware but have distanced yourself from being conscious of your innermost being. His words "isolate, anaesthetized, and unresponsive" suggest that the mind is on rote, asleep, comfortably numb, rather than being fully awake and participating in your thought patterns.

Another aspect of yourself that you are unaware of is how you perceive events and experiences and interpret those situations. Growing up, you were taught to perceive the world by those who shaped your reality. Your family and culture brought forth the meaning, how you function, and the consequences of your perspectives and beliefs and how you view the world and take in information. The consequence is often how you arrive at what you believe to be true.

One of the best studies conducted on our perceptions of what we observe and what we miss in our observations is the book, *The Invisible Gorilla,* by Christopher Chabris and Daniel Simons. Chabris and Simons discovered an important truth:

*Our minds don't work the way we think they do. We think we see ourselves and the world as they really are, but we're actually missing a whole lot.*

If you were to contemplate on the above quote, you might wonder if what you believe and perceive are really true. Perhaps what you believe to be true is often a collective belief or hunch because your beliefs will blind you from seeing the whole picture.

From the research conducted by Chabris and Simon, they suggest that we succumb to everyday illusions. By bringing this information into your awareness, it is their goal to help you understand how your perceptions deceive you and you do not notice the "invisible gorillas" around you and in your own life. Here is one illusion in your life that you can explore. It is the thoughts you tell yourself, the negative self-talk that is not based upon any truths.

# Negative Self-Talk

One of the ways we are not conscious of the mental chatter is what I refer to as negative self-talk. Everyone I know has this and until I point it out, they are unaware of this negative tape playing.

I mentioned earlier that this negative tape is buried deep within us. Throughout my career, I have witnessed the suffering and distress of so many individuals from this destructive mental chatter, and while not self-inflicted, holding onto the negative tape playing from past experiences prolongs the pain and keeps the suffering alive. Becoming conscious of this inner dialogue and what it is saying is another way to watch your thoughts. However, it is important to eradicate this tape as it is unhealthy and can undermine a sense of well-being and inner peace.

Years ago, from a personal experience, I developed a technique to remove this destructive tape. It requires discipline and a constant awareness to catch the tape when it is playing and then an action step to change the tape.

There are many variations of how this tape plays. Each time you catch it playing, you will eventually narrow it down to the root. For many individuals, the root of the tape is usually not being good enough or worthy and this belief is the driver behind most of the choices you make and the decisions you make. Learning my technique is the way to have insight into your negative tape and take control of it by stopping and removing it from your thought process. My technique is called the STOP technique, not a very creative name yet easy to remember.

# The Stop Technique

Here are the steps to the technique. First of all, STOP is not an acronym. It is just the word used when you catch the tape playing. Here is how it works. Let's say the root of your negative tape is that you are not good enough. You choose what I refer to as a launch sentence which could be and should be that you are more than good enough.

Because the tape has been playing for a long time, with many variations, I suggest that people write their launch sentence down and place it in several places, by their bed, one posted on the mirror in the bathroom, one on the dashboard of their car, and one on their computer. The reason for this is when the tape is playing most people do not remember their launch sentence.

It is called a launch sentence because when you catch the tape playing you say STOP and keep saying STOP until you remember your launch sentence. It is best to say your sentence out loud as hearing it reinforces the new programing. From your launch sentence, you pontificate upon the theme of being more than good enough or more than worthy, stating as many variations on that theme as there are in Pachebel's Canon in D.

On the surface, this technique sounds quite simple, yet it is more of a struggle than it appears. To begin with, when the tape is playing, every cell in your body believes what the inner dialogue is saying and that is why it is so hard to remember the launch sentence.

Next, when you are tired and or hungry, the tape plays really loud and this is where some individuals want to give up and surrender to negative chatter. It is at these times to remind yourself that you are merely tired or hungry and that inner chatter is not true and make yourself replace the tape with your launch sentence. I highly recommend that you practice the new programing out loud when in the shower and driving to work to reprogram every cell in your body to believing the new replacement tape. In this way, you are reinforcing the new inner dialogue and carving out a new self-image. Believe it or not, the negative chatter is playing 24/7 even if you are not aware of it or hear it.

One of the ways to catch the tape playing is when someone says something to you and your mind negates and overrides what you heard. For example, I had a client at the C-Suite level in his organization. He was confident and highly skilled. However, whenever one of his peers stated that he did a great job on a project, in his mind he would override the compliment and tell himself it wasn't that great, that he could have done it better.

When I pointed out to him that this was his negative tape playing, he told me that he does this overriding all the time. He then understood that the root of his negative tape was that he was not good enough. I expressed to him each time he overrode a compliment he was reinforcing the tape and believing that underneath all of his accomplishments, he really was not good enough.

Many overachievers have the same issue and I have been told in confidence that at the end of the day, especially when they have been complimented on some achievement, they feel like a fake.

In our waking state, the onslaught of unconscious and excessive negative thoughts robs us of feeling good about ourselves, creating some underlying form of anxiety. Negative thoughts not only generate anxiety, but negative emotions as well.

It is not enough to notice these negative thoughts; you have to become awake to them and detach from believing in what they are saying as they can put you in a fear-based place, debilitating you from being motivated. Instead of merely detaching from them, you implement an action, the STOP technique, to replace the negative thoughts.

How unconscious can you be? Let me share another story. I once worked with a young man who we'll call Michael. Every Monday, we mapped out a plan for him to be successful. Yet, the following Monday, he had failed at overcoming his ingrained patterns of behavior. One Monday morning, I decided it was time for me to take off the velvet glove and use the iron fist to confront him. (For reference, my tag line is: Coaching with an iron fist in a velvet glove.)

When he arrived, he began with the same story I heard every Monday. I stopped him from continuing and told him the following. "Michael, I want you to become conscious of something. I want you to own that you have a tape playing that you are a failure and that you will fail in life. Instead of being unconscious of it, I want you to own it, be conscious of the tape because it is dictating the choices you make and how you perceive yourself."

He sat up and said, "I am choosing to fail life." We explored the root of this tape and after adopting my STOP technique and being conscious of this negative tape, he became very successful in his career.

I have taught the STOP technique for over 20 years and witnessed how effective it is and how it changes lives by quieting the negative mind chatter.

Other notable changes are how perceptions on experiences transform and a general overall outlook on life changes. Using this technique breaks you free from limiting beliefs and can help you become more aware of your biases.

Michael A. Singer, in his book, *The Untethered Soul,* describes what it means to stop in a different way:

*What exactly does it mean 'to stop'? It's something you do inside. It's called letting go. When you let go, you are falling behind the energy that is trying to pull you in it. Your energies inside have power. They are very strong, and they draw your awareness into them … These disturbed energies will draw your consciousness to them. But you do not have to let this happen. You really do have the ability to disengage and fall back behind them. (p. 63)*

I agree with Singer: when we fall behind the energy, we do not give in to its power. Where we differ is from my experience, most individuals are not actively aware that they are being drawn into these disturbed, negative self-talk energies. Because the tape has played for so long, it takes a great deal of effort to become aware of the messages/energies that are playing.

Even though this technique has been most valuable to my clients, I am still met with resistance to doing it when first introduced. The responses are: "This seems silly. It can't be that easy," or "I don't believe the launch sentence, it's not true."

When I hear this struggle, I remind them that every cell in their body believes the negative tape, not the new one, like my executive client from the example earlier. I remind them they have nothing to lose by implementing this technique into their daily lives. Part of the struggle to accepting this technique is the unawareness that the tape is constantly playing even when they are not hearing its undesirable message.

To reach cognitive enlightenment, you need to clear unwanted and unnecessary thoughts. You are working toward controlling your state of consciousness and the STOP technique is a tool to gain self-mastery of your thoughts.

When you reprogram the negative self-talk, you achieve more mental clarity and free yourself from the illusions that have influenced your thinking, which has a direct impact on your stress levels. With this newfound awareness, you are in charge of your thoughts and more conscious of the choices you make and can even question if you are perceiving everything correctly.

Your unconscious cluttered mind-thoughts are being scattered all over the place, creating havoc on you and everyone around you by dredging up negative emotions. Attaining cognitive enlightenment is to rein in and stop the turbulent mind, over-riding your emotions that are stirred up in this whirlwind and shifting to calm your mind and emotional state.

# Chapter Three

## Identities and Projections

How did you become your unique you? What contributed to your self-image and how much do you cling to that self-image?

You have worked hard to become who you are. But what shaped you to become your unique you? Your attitude toward yourself and toward others and the world was primarily shaped from your childhood experiences and reinforced through cultural beliefs and traditions. Carl Jung (1954) stated in his book, *Development of Personality,* that "children are deeply involved in the psychological attitude of their parents" (p. 39).

What you have become, then, is a combination of your parents, and your parents' parents' psychological make-up, what I will refer to as an acquired self. You acquired your unique you through the lens of their upbringing which shaped your upbringing.

Jung explained that "identity derives essentially from the notorious unconsciousness of the small child ... and the things which have the most powerful effect upon children do not come from the conscious state of the parents but from their unconscious background" (p. 41), supporting the notion that you are largely unconscious of who you really are and the acquired self is a persona, not the real you.

If you have an acquired self, is there another self lurking in the shadows? According to James Hollis, there is another self, a natural self:

*The natural self is buried beneath this acquired self, resulting in self-estrangement and sundry symptoms of dis-ease.* (Tracking the Gods, 1995 p. 11)

Hollis states that we "cling to an antiquated self-image" that no longer serves us; thus, we stay stuck in the acquired self, repeating old patterns of behaviors and thought processes often generations old. We think we know ourselves well without thinking about it much. Perhaps this is part of the reason we become unconscious to our thoughts through overidentification with our self-image.

But is this the true essence of who you are? What is the natural self that Hollis is describing? How do you go about getting to a new self-image, a new you? When you cling to this self-image, you are blind to all of who you are, parts that are lying in wait behind the curtain. One way to uncover the natural self is to remove the self from self-image. In this manner, you are beginning to look at what is behind the mask, the persona that you wear.

Another way to discover unknown parts is to look at the people you have a negative charge towards, aspects of personalities and/or behaviors that grate on you, you cannot stand, that irritate you. You often project onto them a myriad of names.

When you are reacting with a charge, this is the door to uncovering aspects of yourself and beginning to know yourself on a deeper level because you are in the land of unknown, unconscious parts of yourself called the shadow.

These are the behaviors excluded from consciousness because you don't want to see yourself in this manner. Rather, you hide behind the mask of self-image of how you want to be seen. You can see these traits in others and often abhor these individuals. But what these others represent is a mirror to you, to traits that you have split off from. Even though you don't see them in yourself, they show up in your life through behavioral flare-ups or projections on others.

Paying attention to who you have a negative charge to, then asking yourself are you this way at times, gives you a glimpse into your own shadow world behind the mask. Let's now look deeper at some of the masks of self-image you might be playing out.

## Archetypes

Jung wrote that "the vast majority of mankind do (sic) not choose their own way, but convention, and consequently develop not themselves but a method and a collective mode of life at the cost of their own wholeness" (Development of Personality, 1954 p. 174), what Kierkegaard called "the mass man." Because of this, you live an unfulfilled life, you notice something missing from your life, or life just seems dull. Perhaps you don't feel like you and long for a more glamorous existence. Instead of digging deep to uncover your natural self that Hollis wrote about, you stay stuck in an acquired self by identifying, unconsciously, with the acquired self-image and self-concept and with specific archetypes.

What are archetypes? Archetypes are universal symbols. For the purposes of this book, I will limit the definition to characters that have a common and recurring representation in the human culture and are in the collective unconscious. Common archetypes are the hero archetype, the villain, the scapegoat, the good mother, the trickster, the mentor, the eternal youth, the whore, the saboteur, and many more that reveal themselves as experiences. You can experience these archetypes through various literary works and films. You also experience them in your own life by looking at your universal personality style. What archetype pulls at you?

Take a moment to sit back and look at your life and personality. Is there an archetype you identify with that is calling to you? How many different archetypes have you taken on in your lifetime? There is no problem with identifying with an archetype unless you overidentify with it. When that occurs, you are no longer in the driver's seat of the decisions you make, from the clothes you choose to wear to your behavior. Let's look at an example.

Let's say you identify with James Bond. If you unconsciously identify with this archetype, you might start drinking martinis, finding night clubs to go to that require you to wear a tuxedo, and you might be so possessed by this archetype you become a womanizer.

Overidentification with an archetype becomes the way you live your life, and it can take over and start dictating your life. If this happens, it is said that you are possessed by the archetype and are no longer in control. Once you are possessed by an archetype, you dis-possess you, and the syzygy takes over. You are no longer even the acquired self and far from uncovering the natural, evolved, transcendent self.

It is certainly all right to revere a certain archetype as long as you are conscious of its drawbacks. For example, Superman is a great hero confronting crime, yet kryptonite is his nemesis and robs him of his power. He is aware of how this aspect of nature is his doom and works hard not to find himself in a situation where there is kryptonite. He is aware that his power is limited and does not fall under the spell of wielding his power over others. He remains humble as his natural self and does not let his superhero powers take control of his life, much like the Joker who became possessed of his mission to destroy Batman.

Because Superman recognizes his own limitations and is not all-powerful is an example of how to engage with an archetype without becoming possessed by it. One of the reasons we admire Superman is because of this awareness that he has limitations.

After his battle with crime, he returns to being the humble and clumsy Clark Kent.

Superman's nemesis is kryptonite. Kryptonite represents nature. Superman is aware he is powerless when it comes to nature. Many individuals in power have lost sight of the fact that nature is all-powerful, destroying cities, and are not humbled when nature has rendered them powerless. These individuals have lost their humility to the one aspect they cannot control.

Engaging an archetype like Superman means we know we have power and we know its limits, especially when dealing with natural forces. He is the perfect archetype for heroic deeds and being humble.

How could this show up in someone's life? If someone is in a powerful position, a leader of an organization, they must be aware of the power of power and like Superman, know its limitations and what their limitations are in that position. They need to show humility where they are powerless. Power can be addicting and can drive the decisions a leader makes, leaving others in their wake. As we all know, power in the wrong hands can have destructive consequences.

A leader possessed by their position and power in that position can take the attitude they have all the answers, and they are always right. This individual does not take advice from others, listening to no one and can become a monster when anyone tries to reason with them. They are possessed by being in power and once possessed, they are no longer in control of themselves.

How do you know when you are in the presence of someone possessed by an archetype? When you find yourself in a relationship with someone who is possessed by an archetype, you will have the feeling you are not encountering an authentic person.

Here is an example. Many years ago, in my psychotherapy days, I had a client who made me feel like I was replaying the characters in the film, *Analyze This*, with Billy Crystal and Robert De Niro, in my own office. In this film, De Niro's role is the Italian gangster archetype. My client had overidentified with an Italian gangster and was behaving in ways much like De Niro's role. During our sessions, I could not discern whether my client had adopted this profession in real life or was more like a child wearing a Halloween costume and was acting and believing he was part of the mafia.

Herein lies the problem: you need to know when to call upon the archetype and when to let it go, much like Superman knows when to be Clark Kent and when to draw upon his identity as Superman. Working with this client, I became so uncomfortable that I had to let him go. I could not discern if he worked for the mafia or not.

How do you know when to engage an archetype? And how can it be useful? In my coaching questionnaire, I ask my clients who are their heroes. When we go over the questionnaire, I delve further into the question, asking them why they chose who they did. Bringing conscious awareness to their heroes and why is moving toward greater self-awareness.

As I learn the appeal of a client's hero, I tell my clients that these are archetypes to call upon during challenging situations or when they are having a hard time making a decision. Doing this exercise allows them to step into the archetype using the power of this representation to guide them through the task that is posing difficulty. They have now become more aware of who they aspire to and how to consciously use the power of the archetype without becoming overidentified with it or possessed by it.

To uncover your natural self, you need to discover what masks you wear, what archetypes you engage or unconsciously live out, and you need to look deeply at your beliefs and the cultural upbringing that shaped your perspectives on life. Are your be-liefs yours? Or are they adopted from multiple generations of indoctrination by your family? Are you able to step back and question your beliefs and perspectives? If so, can you be flexi-ble and be open to another way of thinking about a situation?

All of these questions will address the journey of delving into the acquired self to reach deeply into the area where the natural self resides. It is the process of acquiring new self-knowledge.

# Chapter Four

## Self-Reflection – Taking the Path to Our True Self

How do you become more self-aware and why is it important? Gaining self-awareness moves you into a more conscious state of who you are, your emotions, your fears, your thought patterns, destructive behaviors and insecurities. With this self-awareness, you can begin to question whether you need to hold on to these limiting struggles or let them go to uncover the natural, transpersonal self. How do you begin this journey? Through self-reflection.

Reflecting upon yourself is challenging, especially in these times when you are driven to be distracted from yourself. Social media and playing games on your smart phone all take precedence from sitting and contemplating your inner self. If you were to take time to sit with yourself and reflect upon your day, what you experienced, what you felt in those experiences, how you perceived those experiences, you would be enacting the art of self-reflection.

Instead of practicing the art of self-reflection, you are caught up in two acts: distracting yourself from yourself through a variety of ways, such as your smart phone, or working at accomplishing some feat or deed at work. When you are attempting to finish a deed or mission, you can be unconsciously caught up in the hero's journey.

Taking on a challenge and mastering some feat is admirable. The question is, are you being driven by playing out the hero's journey over and over again or are you able to step back, finding contentment before being driven on to the next feat?

In the last chapter, we explored Superman, a superhero who embarks upon the journey of conquest against crime over and over again. The hero's journey is about deed and imitation, rather than process, as can be observed through the multitude of hero journey films out of Hollywood. The hero's journey is imitated over and over again with different plots and characters. But the role of the hero never changes. It is always the same.

If we move out of this journey, we can move into self-reflection, and self-reflecting is a process of going within and being vulnerable to yourself.

In my dissertation, *Sitting By the Well: A Contemplative Journey Toward Wholeness* (Oct. 2013), I discuss at length the shortcomings of the hero's journey. I mention that the hero's journey is a story about good versus evil, amplifying dualism and polarity. When we are in the realm of judging what is good and bad, right or wrong, we lose sight of what is driving that judgment, beliefs and limiting perspectives. When this happens, we create diversity to such a degree it can often show up in powerful and destructive ways.

Today, we are experiencing that degree of devastation in our own country. The dualistic mindset that is currently running through this country has raised the bar on hatred to such an extent we are experiencing a split like never before, which could lead to unfathomed consequences. This type of split is creating a political nightmare. Instead of unity, this myth is now acted out and perpetuates that one side is good while the other side is evil.

Whether it is happening within a nation or within yourself, prolonging the dualism and judging yourself and situations as good or bad, right or wrong, does not move you toward your true nature. It furthers the split and the need to maintain the mask you have created as your self-image. Perhaps this is the reason Jung wrote in *The Red Book,* "The hero must fail for the sake of our redemption since he is the model and demands imitation" (2009, p. 245). Jung also stated in *The Red Book* that the hero is dead and "if the hero in you is slain, then the sun of the depths rises in you, glowing from afar" (p. 239).

What does that mean, "the sun of the depths rises in you, glowing from afar?" Could it be that once you get out of the realm of judging each situation and experiencing them as good and bad, or any other dualistic judgment, that you might shed light upon a new you, a you that can be free to experience a greater sense of self you have never experienced before bringing a non-judgmental clarity to situations? Could it mean that you transcend the hero only to discover the brilliance in you will arise on the horizon of your life and you will live a uniquely lived life rather than repeating yourself, living a life of imitation?

When you move past the horizon of your present life, you move past your limited self. Living beyond the horizon is living beyond the edge of your world and in the present moment, for that is all you have.

What is being asked of you is to sacrifice that role, the acquired self, with all its limiting beliefs and perspectives to uncover the natural self. Charles Du Bois said it best:

*The important thing is this: To be able at any moment to sacrifice what we are for what we would become.*

What will it take to remove the mask of the acquired self, and step out of the role you have become so accustomed to playing? What is required is a deep self-reflection and an honest scrutiny of your self-concept. In this scrutiny, ask yourself some questions:

1.  Am I happy?

2.  Do I feel fulfilled at the end of the day?

3. What is my attitude upon awakening?

4. Do I feel kindness in me toward other people I encounter?

5. Do I feel a sense of inner peace or am I wrestling with myself and hence, with others?

6. What core emotion or emotions accompany me throughout the day?

7. Do I enjoy life?

8. What is my constant mental chatter saying?

9. Does this mental chatter conjure up irritable emotions?

10. What reactions do I wish I could stop doing?


These are just a few questions to begin self-scrutiny and evaluate yourself and your life. What illusions do you tell yourself? What set of beliefs drive you, your thoughts, emotions, and decisions? I remember when Carole King came out with the song that stated that "*You've got to get up every morning with a smile on your face and show the world all the love in your heart. Then people gonna treat you better.*" Is this not an indoctrination of how to live your life? What if you were to question these first few lines of her song? What if you believed people treated you well whether or not you were showing all the love in your heart? Furthermore, what if you don't feel any love in your heart?

Self-awareness and self-reflection begin by questioning and evaluating the self to the point of questioning what you are being told to believe and how to act. Are not those first few lines in the song suggesting wearing a mask even if that mask isn't you?

If you pay close attention, the first few words, "You've got to," are a demand. How many demands have been made on you to behave, act, and think a certain way? And did you blindly follow those instructions without question? It is time to put yourself under a microscope and look deeply and curiously at every thought, behavior and belief with serious reflection.

Your emotions can drive your thoughts, which can influence how you experience the world. Remember *The Invisible Gorilla?* How does your mask shape your illusions of how you view yourself and others? What emotions are in the driver seat and can you manage your emotions effectively or do they get the most of you? In the next chapter, we are going to look at emotional intelligence and how you can move beyond your emotions being the driver of your daily life.

# Chapter Five

---

## Going Beyond Emotional Intelligence

Conflict is inevitable. Conflicts occur for several reasons, because of communication breakdowns through misunderstandings, misperceptions, and misinterpretations. The absence of conflict does not make for a healthy relationship. What makes a healthy relationship is how the disagreements are resolved.

Conflict is the opportunity to grow in a relationship, deepening the relationship through understanding the other person. A healthy resolution of a conflict can promote a sense of well-being within oneself and with the other person. A stronger bond can ensue because both individuals rose above their own emotional attachments of the small self toward resolving the dispute.

What gets in the way of a healthy resolution of a conflict? Several dynamics can be the culprit. One of the driving factors of disagreements is the need to be right and make the other person wrong. In marriages, when you have to be right and make the other person wrong, you both lose, because after the fact, neither one of you feels very good about the dispute and resolution.

Another circumstance in unhealthy resolution in conflict is avoiding an issue. When this happens, nothing gets resolved because of a lack of talking through the issue, creating a wedge in the relationship. Rather than trying to understand how the other person feels, there is a stalemate, a blockage and the energy around that issue floats between the two individuals for days.

When there is a stalemate in a relationship further action is blocked, leaving the individuals with no options and the act of stonewalling is inevitable. Rather than becoming closer, the individuals distance themselves from each other, as they are at a deadlock. What is the consequence? Blocked energy will result in dis-ease in some form and manner.

Another way conflict can ensue is if there is a problem that has not been resolved. This often occurs in the workplace. When a problem arises, there is a tendency to blame the person, bringing the situation into the blaming/defensive tactic. When there is a problem, often people will attack and blame the other person rather than looking for a solution. Blaming another person usually puts them on the defensive, which breaks down communication and the situation does not get resolved.

In corporations, resolving the problem quickly saves time and money. Blaming an individual does not bring a resolution and can be costly. A better approach is to resolve the predicament, and then seek understanding of where there might have been a misunderstanding, miscommunication, or misinterpretation.

In personal relationships, blaming the other person is not taking responsibility for your own part in the conflict. It is putting all of the breakdown of communication on the other person. The emotion that accompanies the blamer is usually anger and that is why the other person becomes defensive, because they feel threatened by the angry tone and words.

Neuroscience has revealed the brain only knows two states: threat or reward. Furthermore, the brain cannot discern between an actual threat and a perceived threat. When someone is angry and blaming, the person on the other end will feel threatened. Rather than blaming, I have a saying: "You are 100 percent responsible for 50 percent of the conflict," yet blamers do not want to take responsibility for their part in the controversy.

# Five Landmines of Relationships

One final breakdown in communication and unresolved conflict is what I refer to as the five landmines of relationships. The person who has these qualities is 1) in denial that they are any part of a problem, 2) they blame you, others, the world, or the circumstances rather than owning their part of the problem, 3) they usually lie and manipulate, 4) they justify their behavior, and 5) you cannot reason with them.

It is the last behavior that frustrates the person on the receiving end and that person often gets pushed past their limits, tearing their hair out, so to speak, because of the inability to reason with them. You will often lose your self-control because it is so infuriating. If you encounter this type of person, it is best to walk away, as nothing will ever be resolved with this dynamic.

All of the situations mentioned are unhealthy responses to conflict and this is where emotional intelligence comes in. Emotional intelligence is about understanding your emotions, understanding the emotions of others, and the ability to manage your emotions, especially during challenges and adversity.

When you are highly conscious of your emotional states, the next action to take is to manage them rather than act out from them. How do you gain understanding of your emotions? Through greater self-awareness and self-reflection.

A self-reflection exercise is to look back at your interpersonal conflicts and ask yourself how you could have handled the situation better. Were you a blamer? Did you try to avoid the situation? Did you bottle up your emotions and then explode? Did your emotions get the best of you? Developing healthier conflict resolution skills is paramount to attaining cognitive enlightenment. Managing your emotions is a tough challenge and even though you can work on greater understanding of your emotional states, it is not enough.

In my 20-plus years of working with individuals, I have learned that gaining understanding of your emotions requires an awareness of what triggers certain emotions within yourself. Embedded in most triggers are your blind spots and this is why it is so difficult to manage your emotions. Let me tell you a story.

A woman came to me because a colleague told her that her team was afraid of her because she was harsh. She was at the C level of an international, multibillion dollar organization and she wanted to continue to be successful in her position.

When we first met, she told me she didn't see herself as being harsh. She shared with me that throughout her career, her performance reviews had a common area of where she could perform better, in working with how she addresses her team. Even though this was pointed out to her, she didn't know how to change this behavior because it was her blind spot.

Performance reviews often fail the recipient because pointing out a behavior, especially when it is a blind spot, is not enough. Guidance on how to remedy a behavior is the action needed and often requires a coach. Learning what triggers your blind spot is the first step.

In our work together, I discovered what triggered her to become harsh. There is a one-two punch when it comes to blind spots. The first punch is the trigger, the second is what I refer to as the "go-to" style of responding to the trigger. Common "go-to" styles are becoming overly controlling, sarcastic, defensive, avoiding, hostile, emotional, or highly opinionated. In this case, she became hostile in her tone and body language.

One of the biggest challenges of blind spots is that they can be triggered in a variety of ways, which was true for my client. Time and time again, I pointed out to her in our sessions that she was triggered and her exasperated response was, "Why can't I see that?"

The ability to understand and manage emotions is not insurmountable, but requires working with someone who understands and can point out the myriad ways that you will be triggered. My favorite example is the disco ball with all the tiny mirrors. Each mirror represents how many diverse ways your blind spot can be punched.

Understanding your blind spots and the diverse ways they are triggered is going beyond emotional intelligence. It is about enlightening yourself to all of who you are, even when you don't want to look at those aspects of yourself.

## What Lies Behind Misunderstanding, Misinterpretations and Miscommunication?

Many conflicts arise because of some form of breakdown in communication and there are three ways this occurs: misunderstanding, misinterpretation, and miscommunication. Let's look at each one.

How do misunderstandings come about? There are two reasons that come to mind. First, people in general are not good listeners and therefore can miss much of what is said to them. Second, people often speak before thinking about what they are saying and do not say what they really intend.

This happened to me the other day. My sweetheart and I went out to dinner the other night and I brought home leftover pizza. In the morning, I asked him if he wanted the pizza for breakfast. He blurted out with excitement, "That's my favorite!"

I looked at him, puzzled. In all the years I have known him, I did not know this, and I said so. He looked back at me and said, "That's not what I meant."

How many times have you said something and realized that it was not what you meant to say? When this occurs, there is a misunderstanding in the communication. A good approach is to ask for clarification or reflect back what you heard them say. You will be surprised how often you will hear, "That is not what I meant to say."

Misunderstandings can also occur because of one specific behavior – taking what was said too personally. When we take what is said personally, it is ripe for emotions to take over and move you from good communication to furthering the gap of misunderstandings. If you reflect back what was said, you can prevent emotions from taking over. It also gives you time to pause and ponder how best to respond.

Reflecting back is a powerful tool to manage your emotions. A good practice for not taking things personally is to remind yourself that not everything that happens or is said is about you.

Misunderstandings can also occur because not all of the information was heard. You may think you communicated clearly, and you may have; however, the person on the receiving end may have missed some of what you said.

Here is another example of the CIO who came to me for coaching because she wanted to be more effective with her team and less harsh. Working for an international organization was ripe for misunderstandings in communication. I had her take two assessments, the emotional intelligence assessment and the MBTI (Myers Briggs Type Indicator) assessment. On the MBTI she was a J, which means she can make decisions quickly. During our work together, it became apparent that most of her team were Ps, meaning that they needed to gather more and more data and making a decision was a challenge.

A big challenge with Ps is they become hung up on information and often miss the rest of what is being said. For example, if you are telling a P to do A, then B, then C, then D, they may start thinking about B and miss steps C and D.

When communicating, paying attention to the body language can inform you whether you have lost the person. In a meeting with several people, that is much harder to discover. Knowing if you are communicating with a P requires slowing down, asking them to reflect what you have communicated. In this manner, you will know if some of the information is lost or if they took it all in. Reflective listening also reinforces the information and allows you to know if the information was interpreted correctly or not.

Misinterpretations in communication occur for a variety of reasons and can occur because people don't always say what they intend, hence, misunderstanding ensues. Misinterpretations can happen when the listener is jumping to conclusions before hearing all of the information or assuming what the person is going to say and thus missing some. Interpreting information is slanted through your lens of beliefs and your relationship to words, shaping and altering how you hear information. You can also misinterpret information if you get triggered and your emotions take over.

Misinterpreting information can be intentional, as in some scientific findings, to support a bias in the study. It can also be intentional to play ignorant or dumb about a prior conversation. Part of the problem with texting and emails is that the body language and tone are missing, making it easy to misinterpret what is written, leading to miscommunication. For this reason, the use of emojis are helpful to minimize the misinterpretation of information and the emotional tone of the message.

Going beyond emotional intelligence is about gaining a greater understanding of yourself and identifying your triggers. When I conduct my emotional intelligence trainings at organizations, part of the material is devoted to ways to identify your triggers and "go-to" style of responding.

In the earlier example, with the CIO and her team, her trigger was the team taking too long to make a decision during their meetings. When triggered, she became frustrated and her "go-to" style of responding was to be harsh and pounce on her team.

There is a method to help uncover your triggers. Reflect back to a time you became emotionally out of control. Write down the situation and find the defining moment when your emotions were getting the best of you. Write down several of these moments and a common thread between these situations may illuminate where your triggers are as you reflect upon these moments.

I tell my clients there is a kinesthetic charge in the body when they are becoming triggered. The kinesthetic charge is a warning signal that you are being triggered and your emotions could take over the driver's seat instead of you being in control of your emotions.

Catching that moment is when you have a choice to manage your reaction or let the wave of emotions rise up and carry you along for the ride.

Another exercise to uncover your triggers which can also be your blind spots is upon reflection of these moments, ask yourself what you were thinking and feeling. What was your "go-to" style in response to the trigger, as this is the response getting in your own way of managing your emotions. When you are hungry or tired, you are more likely to become triggered. Checking in with yourself periodically about whether you need a snack or a break to refresh yourself can minimize being triggered.

And the ultimate question to advance yourself beyond emotional intelligence is how could you have responded differently? This question is crucial to getting out of your box. When I helped the

CIO connect the dots of what triggered her, I asked her what she could do differently. There was a long silence. Finally she said she didn't know. I told her to start her meeting, lay out the parameters for whatever was to be decided upon, tell her team she would be back in 25 minutes and she expected an answer.

She said, "Can I do that?" I responded, "Absolutely, and they want you to leave." In her box was a belief that she had to stay with her team. Before you can get out of your box, you need to understand what your box is comprised of, which is mostly your beliefs and perspectives. This is why finding a way to respond differently is so challenging, because you are relying on your own resources, your box.

Going beyond emotional intelligence is more than managing and understanding your emotions. It is about uncovering triggers and blind spots, learning what your box is made of, and coming up with what I tell my clients is a "never before thought of" response.

Until you identify what triggers you, you will not be able to stop the response that can break down communication and enlarge conflicts. In my training, I suggest different mindfulness practices. Mindfulness practice promotes flexibility in the brain, lengthens the time for you to choose a different response when triggered, promotes resilience so you are less likely to take things personally, and enhances focus, creativity, and calmness. Dan Siegal, a neuroscience researcher, stated:

*Being mindful, having mindful awareness is often defined as a way to intentionally pay attention to the present moment without being swept away with judgments.*

In the next chapter, we are going to explore the practice of mindfulness further. All of my clients that have adopted a daily mindfulness discipline have noticed a difference in their lives. There is a space between, a small moment where they are more conscious of not responding or choosing a different response to their triggers.

# Chapter Six

## Mastering Fear Through Mindfulness

In the early days of my career, someone asked me what I specialized in as a psychotherapist. As I thought about my current client load, I realized that underlying everyone's issues was fear. Coming out from my reverie, I told this individual, "I specialize in fear." He looked at me with wide eyes and said, "Then everyone needs to see you!"

Walking away, I pondered this realization I had just come upon. Fear embodies a wide range of emotions, from mild dread to extreme anxiety or terror. At the base of all fear is a loss of courage. There are two types of fear: physical fear and moral fear. For our purposes, I am going to only address moral fear.

What is moral fear? It is a fear to be yourself, a fear to speak up, and a fear to confront others, especially if they are being disrespectful to you. Often what accompanies fear is not only a lack of courage but a lack of self-confidence as well. The image that arises for me is the cowardly lion in *The Wizard of Oz*.

*The Cowardly Lion of Oz* is the 17th book in the series of Oz books written by L. Frank Baum and his successors. In this story, the lion tells Dorothy that being a coward is his greatest sorrow, and makes his life very unhappy. He believes he is inadequate because of his fear, especially since a lion is supposed to be "the king of beasts." What the lion does not understand is it takes courage, and courage is about taking action in those moments when faced with fear.

Let's explore moral fear a bit deeper in conjunction with courage and yourself. Are you like the cowardly lion? Do you lack the courage to assert yourself? Do you find it challenging to confront someone?

If I were to hold a workshop for those who avoid confrontation, I would not be able to find a convention center large enough to hold all the individuals who are confrontation avoidant. I can't tell you how many people I have worked with that wish they could speak up for themselves and say what they want to express, yet remain silent because of some fear.

A common occurrence for not speaking up is when someone is disrespectful to you in some manner, whether it is through an action or words. Every time you do not address a disrespectful action or words, you are setting yourself up for this behavior to continue.

One of the ways someone can be disrespectful is in the tone in which the individual is speaking. I often give my clients phrases to practice empowering them to speak up. For example, if someone is using an angry tone, I tell my clients to tell them, "I am willing to listen to what you have to say but not in that tone." My clients love this phrase and it is easy for them to use.

Once you start speaking up, it will become easier. You might have to think about past situations and come up with phrases to use. Practice saying your phrases out loud to reinforce your courage. By stepping into the situation and speaking up, you may prevent any misunderstandings and/or miscommunications. Stepping into a situation is also an opportunity to clear up misunderstandings and miscommunications.

When you hold your emotions in rather than expressing yourself, those emotions create inner turmoil, they eat at you, they can consume you and metastasize into gross proportions where you eventually blow up and become aggressive.

When this occurs, you have often lost sight of the root issue and the other person can be blindsided by the eruption. If this occurs, you are not being assertive. Rather, you are being aggressive, like the king of beasts' roar. One of the biggest challenges I face in coaching is helping individuals understand that when you assert yourself, you are not being aggressive. Being aggressive is when your emotions get the best of you and you erupt, using aggressive body language and tone.

Addressing issues promptly allows both individuals to move on or not. Asserting yourself and finding your voice is empowering. Cognitive enlightenment is about not continuing to live with inner/moral sorrow and feelings of being inadequate. It is also about having a realistic perspective on yourself. When faced with a threat, the cowardly lion protected Dorothy. He did not let his fear immobilize him. He felt the fear and stepped into the situation anyway. What he didn't understand is that fear is not the culprit, it is not taking action when faced with the fear.

What prevents someone from confronting a situation? The usual response is they do not like conflict. I have discussed already the consequences of avoiding a situation. It does not solve the miscommunication between the individuals and nothing is ever resolved.

The other day, a client told me about a situation that arose between herself and a colleague. She asked me if she should tell her colleague how she felt. Absolutely! If my client did not, she would hold on to the situation, it would eat at her, and the disturbing feelings would metastasize.

Avoiding confrontation was my client's norm. We worked on developing assertiveness because by not doing so, she lived with tremendous anxiety driven by the turbulent mind chatter around uncontrollable events created by others. What you have control of is, much like the cowardly lion, having the courage to feel your fear and take action.

A key goal with my client as we worked together was about developing her courage to speak up when needed. Anais Nin said it well when she wrote, *"Life shrinks or expands in proportion to one's courage."*

Shrinking is not taking action and speaking up for yourself. Expanding is feeling the fear and stepping into the situation, overcoming your fear.

What is the upside to confronting? Pointing out a behavior that is unhealthy when presented in a compassionate way is an opportunity to bring awareness to that person. They can either grow from this information or not. How the individual responds to feedback also gives you information about that person. If the person is receptive, then you both can move on. If the person becomes defensive, you do not have to engage further. You can reflect back their defense, which doesn't mean you agree, and then move on. You do not have to engage in an additional conflict if they become defensive.

With this approach, you have nothing to lose by addressing the situation and can move past the issue. Your mission is to face your fear, address the issue and move past without further reminiscence.

Adopting a mindfulness practice will assist you in overriding your emotions so you can present the information calmly. A mindfulness practice also brings more clarity to the mind because you are actively working toward quieting the mind chatter. Allowing space and silence, you become less impulsive with this practice, where you can be more conscious of your responses and less reactionary. In this space of silence, Rumi wrote, *"Listen to the silence, it has so much to say."*

Mastering the mind through a mindfulness practice will facilitate cognitive enlightenment. And it takes courage to endure putting yourself under the microscope for self-discovery, bringing unconscious content to the surface. What you discover can be painful but not as painful as going through life like the cowardly lion, sad, miserable, and delusional.

Fear immobilizes you and, like my client, perpetuates anxiety. What is the opposite of fear? I ask my clients this often and they are always surprised when I tell them the opposite of fear is love.

When you lack courage and self-confidence, does that mean you do not love yourself? Do you not feel worthy of love? And more importantly, are you not in touch with your heart? When you do not speak up, you are going against your heart and it is a sort of soul death. Loving yourself is about honoring your heart.

If we look at the origins of the word courage, it is "cor" the Latin word for heart. Courage is and comes from the heart. When we consider what courage originally meant, it was to speak your mind from your heart honestly and openly.

What needs to be explored is: Where did the origin of your fear come from for you not to speak openly and honestly from your heart? That is putting yourself under the microscope for self-discovery. Before being vulnerable with others, become vulnerable to yourself. Get in touch with your heart. Listen to your heart. Leave all self-judgment behind you and be open to what Rumi wrote. The silence has much to tell you. During this mindfulness practice, the goal is to calm your mind in silence and when an emotion arises, do not become attached to the feeling, just take note and let it go. Be open to whatever arises that might give you a glimpse into the origin of your moral fears and let them go as they no longer serve you.

Many benefits of a mindfulness practice have already been mentioned. The mission is to become more adaptable to change, have the courage to make changes in yourself, in your behaviors, beliefs, what you tell yourself, and changing the negative self-talk. Jon Kabat-Zinn, creator of the mindfulness based stress reduction program, defines mindfulness as:

*"a state of heightened alertwareness (sic), a form of non-judgmental and non-reactive attention to experiences occurring in the present moment, including bodily sensations, emotions, thoughts as well as environmental stimuli, such as scents, sounds, etc."*

In this practice, you notice without responding. Developing mindfulness is about being consistent with your practice. What is required of you is a high level of integrity to maintain a daily discipline and motivation. I am going to repeat a saying: If you have the awareness of what you want to change and the intention to change it, and work on it daily, the change that you seek will manifest. Remember, your thought processes shape your reality. What you are trying to achieve is a reprogramming of your mind and gaining a deeper understanding of yourself. Making changes in your long-held beliefs and being aware that they are just a perspective is a most arduous process.

What prevents you from adopting some form of mindfulness practice? The most common excuse I hear is, "I don't have time."

You do have time. There is so much to distract you from yourself, social media, texting, gaming, and so much more. A mindfulness practice is something that can be done for one minute every hour and there are apps that can give you a mindfulness chime, reminding you it is time to take one minute to be mindful. During that one minute, you can focus on your breathing. With each breath, be mindful of the inhale and the exhale.

Another one-minute practice is yawning. I know that sounds odd, but the physiological benefits of yawning are several. Yawning relaxes the mind. When you relax your mind, you will be more focused on the task you were working on. When you restore your focus, you improve cognitive functioning. Yawning improves your memory and lowers stress levels. And it enhances introspection and consciousness. All of these benefits will bring about greater self-awareness.

Earlier I explored negative self-talk. If you look at the cowardly lion, his negative thoughts made his life miserable. When you worry or have negative thoughts, they reinforce the belief you have about yourself and create a toxic environment within yourself and for those around you. Ultimately, you increase your stress levels with the negative thoughts and worry. Having a daily mindfulness practice will decrease the stress, bringing about a greater sense of calm to go through your day.

I want to mention an app that I have found to be most effective. It was developed by HeartMath and is called Inner Balance. Using this app, you are working with your breath to bring about emotional coherence and reduce stress levels. I highly recommend investigating this app. You can download it onto your phone.

A client of mine uses it for 10 minutes before starting his workday. He reported to me that after only one week, he felt less stressed at work and managing his emotions was easier. The other day he shared with me that when thoughts of an employee entered his mind during the Inner Balance session, the coherence meter went red.

This was great insight into how another person can disrupt inner peace. He gained more self-awareness, yet he did not know how to prevent the meter from going into the red.

He shared with me that this individual is very arrogant and it grates on his nerves. I pointed out to him that he is letting this person disturb his inner peace. I also reminded him how everything outside of him is out of his control. The only thing in his control are his thoughts, actions and words. Together, we explored ways for him to transcend the stress this individual caused him so his inner peace would not be disrupted by the posturing of arrogance.

In the next chapter is a story that amplifies a journey toward cognitive enlightenment by challenging beliefs and the internal struggle that ensues. Often, when your world turns upside down, so to speak, you can jump out of your box from the experience and transform your life.

# Chapter Seven

## Derek's Cognitive Enlightening

In the chapter about heroes, I made reference to my dissertation, *Sitting By the Well: A Contemplative Journey Toward Wholeness*. My research led me to England and Wales, where I was to visit the sacred wells and experience them personally.

Before I embarked upon this journey, I learned about the loric legends of these wells. Many of the stories were about transformation. When you take on the task of making changes in your life, you are in the midst of healing and transforming your life.

Here is the story of Derek, a taxi driver in Pembrokeshire, Wales whose unconscious and deep-rooted beliefs were transformed in one day. Derek's story ties together all of the material presented in this book thus far. A story like Derek's amplifies how unconscious we are of deep-seated beliefs, biases, and perspectives and how we try to avoid the discomfort of them being confronted. It also illuminates how quickly a conflict can ensue even between two individuals who are on the same mission. I will weave into the telling of this story what to take note of for you to ponder upon more deeply to amplify the point being made.

Pembrokeshire, Wales was the last leg of my journey visiting sacred wells. When I arrived at the train station in Pembrokeshire, I told the driver, Derek, that I needed someone to drive me around to visit five sacred wells the next day. He told me that he has lived in Pembrokeshire his entire life and never visited any sacred wells, so he agreed to pick me up and help me find them. I handed him a list of the wells I wanted to visit and the villages where they were located before he left so we could be efficient with our time the following day.

He picked me up promptly and off we went. Unlike England, where the sacred wells are clearly marked, in this area of Wales, only one well was well known. The rest proved to be a grueling test of search, search again, retrace our steps, and asking locals if they knew the whereabouts of the sacred well.

Here is the story of two of the five wells, where Derek had to confront deep-seated beliefs that first caused him discomfort and finally resulted in an inner transformation of letting them go.

I too made a shift in my perspective. When we did not find the first well, I was baffled and surprised by how upset Derek was about not finding it. Discovering that his interest in these wells was more than helping a visitor with her dissertation, my focus shifted from my personal experience regarding sacred wells to experiencing the wells through Derek's perspective coming into contact with them.

It was a defining moment where my knowledge and understanding of sacred wells became less important than encountering the wells through Derek's felt experience (p. 79).

It is important to note that an aspect of cognitive enlightenment is a form of removing oneself personally from an experience to the perspective of nonjudgmental witnessing.

## Encounter with a Belief

The sacred well, Ffynnon Fair, (ffynnon is the Welsh word for well) resides in the small village of Maenclochog and it is at this well Derek had his first confrontation with a belief.

When we found the natural spring of water bubbling up from the ground, I tasted the water, which had a sweetness to it. In my research about sacred wells, the loric legends are often about a transformation occurring in the individual just from drinking the sacred water. I drank from many of the sacred wells during my travels as a form of ritual, honoring the legends.

After enjoying the cool fresh water, I looked up at Derek and he had a surprised look on his face. I suggested he have a drink from this natural spring but he walked away, his discomfort showing in his face. It seemed my suggestion stimulated some unconscious process "which were intensified from my drinking from the spring" (Fouts, 2013, p. 80). Here is an important clue about discovering unconscious beliefs.

When you are observing someone's behavior or action that makes you uncomfortable (and it isn't unethical or breaking the law), you are probably bumping into one of your deep-rooted beliefs. Tracey, in his book, *Edge of the Sacred,* wrote that "the contacts with the depths requires a certain psychic fluidity, a shift in identity, and a loosening of the tie to the rational mind" (Tracey, 2009, p. 119). When you are uncomfortable, something within your depths is being stirred, and that is an opportunity to question what it is, to look deeper into yourself.

Beliefs and perspectives can keep you rigid in your thinking. Many individuals feel threatened when their beliefs and perspectives are challenged or they encounter someone who does not think and believe like they do.

These are defining moments. You can become curious about the discomfort you are experiencing. You can ask yourself, where did this come from? You have a choice to be open to a different perspective or not.

As Tracey suggests, you need to be fluid and able to let go of an identity that has been held up by your beliefs, allowing yourself to change and adapt to new thoughts, beliefs, and ideas. Derek was being confronted with this opportunity to taste the waters from this sacred well.

Sometimes persistence is required when an individual is struggling with the discomfort of opening up. I urged him again to taste the water. Immediately, "another shift transpired within him. Derek moved from a place of fear and resistance to almost plunging into this small spring" (Fouts, 2013, p. 80). I witnessed Derek opening up as he tasted the fresh water, becoming enamored and hopeful with finding our first well together, Ffynnon Fair.

Transformation can happen rapidly and with my urging, Derek took the leap into dismantling his beliefs. "Jung (1959) wrote, 'Our conscious intentions are continually disturbed and thwarted, to a greater or lesser degree, by unconscious intrusions whose causes are at first strange to us" (p. 104).

Your conscious intentions can be the roadblocks to keeping you stuck in your beliefs. Derek's conscious intention was to move on and avoid feeling the discomfort. I do not know what went through his mind after my second attempt to get him to taste the water, but something in the unconscious moved him past his fear to taking that first drink.


## Transformation at Ffynnon Llanllawer


The same villager who helped us find Ffynnon Fair gave us directions to the next sacred well. She was adamant and repeated twice that when we arrive at the village, to stop at the pub and ask for directions.

The drive took us up into the beautiful Welsh hills before descending into the village, arriving at the only pub in town. I ran into it while Derek walked up the street to ask directions from a gentleman we drove by while arriving into town.

The lovely pub, whose tables were decorated with tablecloths featuring two shades of pink/rose lace, was owned by a woman who knew exactly where the well existed because her parents were buried in the chapel that is up the hill from the well. She said to drive up to a chapel, go just past, and there was the well. When I came out of the Pub, I saw Derek still conferring with the Welsh chap. When we got back into the car to compare notes, I found it intriguing that the chap never mentioned a chapel while my informant was adamant that the well resided by a chapel (Fouts, 2013, p. 82).

It is important to note here, perspectives come into play on how we take in information. It is also note-worthy how my writing is emphasizing the importance of inquiring at the pub and how Derek sought a different source even though both of us were told to stop there. Here is where we can see how interpretation of information can shape our perceptions leading to biases and beliefs and resulting in potential conflict which Derek and I experienced once we compared the directions we were told.

Let me ask you to ponder this: Is my emphasis on the chapel already forming an impression on you which could be shaping your opinion and perspective? Could you become biased toward one set of directions over another if you heard Derek's version after hearing mine?

Furthermore, because we have developed a relationship through this book, you might be biased toward my version since you are getting to know me and have just been introduced to Derek.

We tend to "side" with the person we know rather than a stranger. We can also shape a bias because when we communicate, we often add emphasis to certain words, and we also can leave out information. Here is a question to ask yourself. Are you being swayed into believing the chapel is a crucial element to finding the well, especially since the woman had a personal connection to it?

I was, and immediately moved into the positioning that the directions given to me were correct and Derek's were incorrect. Taking this stance can lead to conflict. A better attitude is one of not being attached, allowing the journey to unfold while searching for the next well.

Being a small village, both sets of directions told us to drive up the long, narrow steep road. "Derek was skeptical because he could not fathom a well, a natural spring of water welling up from under the ground on a hill" (Fouts, p. 82). He stated that water flows down, not up.

At the previous well, it appeared that water was running into the natural spring rather than bubbling up from the ground as it was so small. Water tends to defy nature. As a solid it expands and floats, defying gravity. I often use water to help individuals I coach understand how to get out of their box because of the paradoxical nature of water. While we drove, I pondered how the unconscious resembles the characteristics of water.

At Ffynnon Fair, something from Derek's unconscious bubbled up from the depths within him to become more fluid to taste the water of this sacred well bursting through long-held beliefs.

Eventually we found the chapel and now had to find the well. Derek acquiesced to my directions as he deemed it was my dissertation and field of study. As we approached the obvious well, "Derek was full of child-like wonder and delight when we climbed up the hill and discovered this well. A strong emotion came gushing up from deep within him and, throwing up his hands in the air, he proclaimed, 'Praise God. We found it!' Something was happening to this 52-year-old meek, non-emotive, soft spoken man" (Fouts, p. 85). I was in the midst of witnessing such a powerful inner transformation in Derek that it was a moment of enlightenment.

Caught up in his own sacred moment, Derek walked back to the car, telling me he would be right back. He returned with two coins, one for each of us to throw into the well.

The urge to engage in ritual often begins with an impulse to express oneself where words are inadequate and only action can convey the deep inner feeling. Derek's felt experience into unknown territory was opening him up to ritual and initiating him into an expansion of consciousness (Fouts, p. 83).

What is essential here is that he had become part of a tradition that resides within all of us, called the collective unconscious. Often our beliefs are from multiple generations of rituals from which we act upon without questioning.

In the chapter that talked about archetypes, I wrote that archetypes are universal symbols. For the purposes of this book, I will limit the definition to characters that have a common and recurring representation in the human culture and are in the collective unconscious. With this said, the sacred well is an archetype in the collective unconscious in which Derek became caught up in re-enacting the tradition of throwing a coin into the well and making a wish. Jung (1959) wrote about the power of the archetype that explains Derek's reaction.

*The archetype is pure, unvitiated nature, and it is nature that causes man to utter words and perform actions whose meaning is unconscious to him, so unconscious that he no longer gives it a thought (p. 210).*

It is critical to note how all of us are shaped by cultural rituals and the beliefs associated with these collective actions. More importantly, unconscious strong emotions, as witnessed in Derek, are directly related to the power of these beliefs. Derek's experience illuminates the power of archetypes and the emotional connections that arise when in the midst of the image.

Corbett (2012) suggested,

*The archetypes are ... pieces of life itself — images that are integrally connected to the living individual by the bridge of emotions. That is, they are real processes ... the archetypes inform our psychological and spiritual development (p. 46).*

Derek was thrown into an unknown and unconscious inner territory that took him by surprise. His cognitive enlightening was when he opened himself up to experience discomfort in unknown territory and then dropped all pretense around his tightly held beliefs.

Archetypes can do that to us and with a flood of emotions can awaken ourselves to expand rather than shrink. His next step was to allow the emotions to be the bridge back to imagination and a newfound self. Close-minded people struggle with beliefs outside of their own. It took the power of the archetype to break through Derek's limited position where new knowledge could be grasped.

Remember our definition of cognitive enlightenment:

*The process of paying attention to our mental thought processes, recognizing thought patterns that are driven by perspectives and beliefs, having awareness of our biases and awakening to and being open to choosing and navigating our thinking to be unattached to our ways of perceiving and transcend ourselves to utilize emotional and spiritual insight to create a higher and untethered thought process to bring about inner peace.*

Moments of inner peace do happen. Becoming free of limiting thoughts and beliefs is a process of transcending ourselves.

Derek picked me up the following day to take me to the train station. There was a pleasant silence between us. At the station, he told me he was going to continue searching for the sacred wells in Wales and to send him names of ones I wanted him to find.

When we have a moment of cognitive enlightenment, we want to hold on to that experience as a way to re-activate the feelings. Yet once we break through and transcend, we need to take on new and different experiences to challenge our perspectives and beliefs and continue transcending ourselves.

# Chapter Eight

## Epilogue

Now, to share a story of my own journey toward cognitive enlightenment. As I mentioned, about 14 years ago, when the Dalai Lama touched his heart asking why would he let the Chinese in there to disturb his inner peace, I was motivated to not allow anyone or anything to disturb my inner peace. I was hungry for inner peace and as a highly disciplined individual, I knew if I kept at it, I would succeed.

Do you realize how many times a day we let something outside of ourselves disrupt our inner sense of well-being? We let strangers disrupt us. We let the weather disrupt us. We let just about everything and everybody stir up emotions that disrupt us. I became extremely aware of this as I started my journey. Putting myself under the microscope to free myself from inner turmoil threw me into the muck and mire of how by our own doing we create turbulence in our minds. Here is my discovery of how I disrupted my own inner peace and well-being.

## Carrying Problems Up the Mountain

Each morning, I hike up the mountain before going to work. One morning, I became aware of turbulent mind chatter. If I have a problem with someone, I discovered I was working out how to discuss the issue with that person when hiking up the mountain in the morning rather than enjoying the hike and the views.

One morning, I stopped hiking and said to myself, "Why are you carrying this person up the mountain with you? Stop it! He is disrupting your inner peace."

Yep, mind chatter. Conversations in our heads. Was this individual even thinking about me? Probably not. As trite as it may sound, I learned that I held counsel with myself every morning in my head while hiking up the mountain, turning what could have been a peaceful morning into mental debates. I was so consumed by these conversations that I was not being present with the beauty surrounding me.

Even though I now had this awareness, the habit was so strong I found myself on many mornings caught up repeating conversations that didn't have to happen. With this acute awareness, I struggled to stop the mind chatter as it had become an ingrained habit.

I realized that very few of these inner conversations I had with myself ever actually happened. What a waste of emotional energy. Eventually I conquered this issue, only to discover more challenges. It is a choice as to what we have going on in our heads. And the emotions tied up with the mental chatter can be overwhelming and disruptive.

Each morning it became easier to not metaphorically carry someone up the mountain. Letting go of these conversations, however, was replaced by another mental exercise. Yes, we can become attached to the mental chatter rather than allow the silence and space to surround us. The replacement exercise was the "I am not …" exercise. I would go through my various roles and titles and take them away. I would say, *I am not Melinda. I am not a mother. I am not a psychotherapist. I am not an executive coach.* And so on. I would push to let go of every title and role, to strip away to arrive at "I am."

I do not recommend this exercise to everyone. I share it with you because it was a process to remove my ritual of morning mental conversations while hiking up the mountain. If I did not cling to any identity, I thought it would cleanse me of holding onto situations to process while I hiked.

It worked. Before my first step, I would take a deep breath in and out, relieving myself of the identities and clear my mind preparing mental space for silence. The peacefulness I experienced on my hikes was transformational. I became more aware of the subtleties of the area I thought I knew so intricately and the hiking was easier without all the mental barrage going on.

My progress on cognitive enlightenment was slow going. Beyond beliefs and perspectives are ingrained habits. These habits can often be unconscious, making it harder to eradicate them. How many of you talk to yourself, or make inner commentaries about this or that, judgments of others and situations that don't really concern you? We all do and it can be an ongoing inner chatter on just about everything and anything. A large part of disrupting our inner peace is resisting what is rather than accepting it.

## Inner Turmoil

Being aware of all the intricacies that disrupt you is about having constant awareness. When you catch yourself, stop. Just stop. As you progress, you can catch it sooner and move on from attachment of that moment.

My mind chatter quieted down in the mornings; however, one morning, without the mind chatter, there was a sensation in my chest of inner turmoil. No inner conversation but I could feel the inner struggle about which action to take on a situation. With this awareness, I did not like the discomfort and one morning I said to myself, "Quit! You know the right choice. You don't have to wrestle with yourself. You're wasting energy and disrupting your inner peace!" The next few days, when I felt the wrestle, I stopped and knew the truth of how to proceed.

We all make situations harder than they need be, often because of ego. If we let ego get out of the way, we could probably attain cognitive enlightenment much faster and easier.

Moving away from the inner turmoil was another aspect of becoming more in touch with my truer self, a self that knew the right action from the beginning. When we quiet the mind chatter, the judgments, and let go of being disrupted by the things we have no control over, we can simplify our lives and hear truth coming through to us much louder. A quiet mind facilitates knowing the right decision to make and it comes to you swiftly and clearly.

As the years progressed, I became better at my discipline and could catch myself quickly. I am sure you have all heard about peeling back the layers of the onion. Gaining greater self-awareness and working toward cognitive enlightenment is just that: removing layers of the self, the acquired self, to arrive at a more peaceful natural self.

Now I have to humble myself to admit to one area where I allowed complete strangers to disrupt my inner peace. This was far down on the layers I had already peeled away, as I was making progress.

## Possessed by an Archetype

Normally, I am a very patient person, except when it comes to driving the car. Once behind the wheel, I discovered I became possessed by an archetype, and turned into Cruella De Vil, from the movie "101 Dalmatians." Yes, she is an archetype who is a monster toward anyone in her way, and her driving is reckless and ruthless.

When we work toward cognitive enlightenment, we have to be honest with ourselves, even our shadow selves. It's not easy to admit to being possessed by an archetype, especially one that is so disgustingly horrid. Here is what I uncovered.

When sitting behind another car at a red light, when the light turned green I would say things like, "How green does the light have to be?" Or, "Are you having a hard time finding the gas pedal?"

I live in a rural area and the commute to my office takes about 10 minutes. In those few minutes Cruella De Vil took over and the words out of my mouth were horrible and I became all worked up while driving.

One day, when sitting behind a car at the light, it dawned on me how I was letting these drivers disrupt my inner peace and for what? Wasn't my goal to not let anyone or anything disrupt my inner peace? Here I was, letting something so insignificant disrupt me.

It wasn't their intention to evoke these emotions. In fact, as I looked at the driver next to me, he turned and smiled, obviously not hell-bent upon hitting the gas as soon as the light turned green.

When we say, "Something dawned on me" we are in a moment of opportunity for cognitive enlightenment. In that dawning, there is an opening where light can be let in for self-awareness. I realized I was acting like Cruella De Vil and that, even before I was sitting behind someone at the light, she had already possessed me. The minute I pulled out from the garage, she was in control.

How did this happen? I wondered. Looking back, it stemmed from my childhood. My mom was possessed by Cruella De Vil as well when she drove us to school and back. She was a hellion behind the steering wheel. Here is an example of how our upbringing shapes us unconsciously. Yet, it felt like there was something more lurking behind being possessed by Cruella.

## Justifying Our Actions

When we put ourselves under the microscope, we need to delve into the depths and listen to the silence that has much to say. Once the dawning appears, we can close up that opening and become content to live comfortably numb, or we can allow the dawning to shed light on unconscious content.

Looking at my actions while driving, I told myself I was justified because I can't stand stupidity and not paying attention to when the light turns green is being unaware and stupid.

Listen up now, as what I am going to reveal is crucial. I was justifying my actions and guess what, we all do. Instead of changing, we hold on to an action or behavior and justify ourselves.

In my work, I see this all the time. Justifying behaviors and feelings keeps you stuck in old patterns. When I looked closely at my justification, I realized this too was an aspect of the Cruella De Vil archetype. She called her thugs imbeciles, feeling justified in treating them poorly. Sad to admit, but she really had a hold on me at times.

Once you realize that you are possessed by an archetype, you need to look at all aspects of how and where it shows up in your life. With this awareness, you will no longer unconsciously act out this character and can choose to remove the behaviors that go along with the archetype. When I removed being possessed by Cruella by making it conscious, my driving slowed down, and I enjoyed the inner silence on my way to work.

More than that, I untethered myself from being charged by ignorance or any other qualities that I deemed undesirable, resulting in disrupting my inner peace.

These examples on my journey are merely highlights of all that I experienced and am experiencing. They are here to illuminate and perhaps resonate something within you. Being transparent with yourself can facilitate your path toward cognitive enlightenment.

Attaining cognitive enlightenment is a life-long journey. The path to transforming your life is endless; there is no end to reach. It is about peeling away the trappings of beliefs, perspectives, biases, endless mind chatter and judgments that cling to you like chains.

I hope from telling Derek's story and my story, you are motivated to delve into self-discovery and cherish each moment when you have a cognitive enlightenment experience.

Will you falter? Of course. I still do. Be gentle with yourself and love yourself. At the moment you are conscious of inner peace being disrupted outside of your control, stop. Take charge and let go of the chain that binds you to the disruption. It is in the awareness when change takes place.

One final word from the Dalai Lama:

*We can never obtain peace in the outer world until we make peace with ourselves.*

I send you blessings on your journey. Find your inner peace and we will be one person closer to world peace. Share your experiences with others as you move along your path. Your story can encourage others to desire inner peace through cognitive enlightenment.

# References

Chabris, C. & Simons, D. (2011). *The invisible gorilla: How our intuitions deceive us.* N.Y. N.Y.: Crown Publishers

Fouts, M. (2013). *Sitting by the well: A contemplative journey toward wholeness.* Ann Arbor, MI: ProQuest LLC.

Fouts, M. (2015). *Increasing emotional intelligence through observing thought waves.* LinkedIn.

Hillman, J. (1983). *Archetypal psychology: A brief account.* Putman, CT: Spring Publications.

Hollis, J. (1995). *Tracking the gods: The place of myth in modern life.* Toronto Canada: Inner City Books.

Jung, C. G. (1954). The development of personality. In H. Reid, M. Fordham, G. Adler, W. McGuire (Eds.) (R.F.C. Hull Trans.) *The collected works of C.G. Jung.* (5th edition, volume 17). Princeton, NJ: Princeton University Press.

Jung, C. G. (1959). The archetypes and the collective unconscious. In H. Reid, M. Fordham, G. Adler, W. McGuire (Eds.) (R.F.C. Hull Trans.) *The collected works of C.G. Jung.* (10th edition, volume 9). Princeton, NJ: Princeton University Press.

Jung, C. G. (2009). *The red book.* NY, NY: W. W. Norton & Company.

Kabat-Zinn, J. (2013). *Full catastrophe living: Using the wisdom of your body and mind to face stress, pain, and illness.* NY, NY: Bantam Books.

Kahneman, D. (2011). *Thinking, fast and slow.* NY, NY: Farrar, Straus, and Giroux.

Singer, M. A. (2007). *The untethered soul: the journey beyond yourself.* Noetic Books. Institute of Noetic Sciences: New Harbinger Publications.

Tracey, D. (2009). *Edge of the sacred: Jung, psyche, earth.* Einsiedeln, Switzerland: Daimon Verlag.

HEIN HERZ FÜR AUTOREN A HEART FOR AUTHORS À L'ÉCOUTE DES AUTEURS MIA KAPΔIA ΓIA ΣYΓΓP
HJÄRTA FÖR FÖRFATTARE UN CORAZÓN POR LOS AUTORES YAZARLARIMIZA GÖNÜL VERELIM SZÍV
CUORE PER AUTORI ET HJERTE FOR FORFATTERE EEN HART VOOR SCHRIJVERS TEMOS OS AUTO
HENRZÓINKÉRT SERCE DLA AUTORÓW EIN HERZ FÜR AUTOREN A HEART FOR AUTHORS À L'ÉCOU
CORAÇÃO BCEЙ ДУШОЙ K ABTOPAM ETT HJÄRTA FÖR FÖRFATTARE Á LA ESCUCHA DE LOS AUTOF
AUTEURS MIA KAPΔIA ΓIA ΣYΓΓΡΑΦΕΙΣ UN CUORE PER AUTORI ET HJERTE FOR FORFATTERE EEN H
YAZARLARIMIZA GÖNÜL VERELIM SZÍVÜNKET ZÓINKÉRT SERCE DLA AUTORÓW EIN HERZ FÜR
VOOR SCHRIJVERS TEMOS OS AUTORES CORAÇÃO BCEЙ ДУШОЙ K ABTOPAM ETT HJÄRTA FÖF

# The author

With a Ph.D. in psychology and over 20 years
in private practice helping individuals and
organizations, Melinda Fouts has crafted unique
skills and techniques to bring about greater self-
awareness. Her passion and mission has been to
guide those she works with toward uncovering
areas that limit them, disrupting their inner peace
and living a truly fulfilled life. Living in the Rocky
Mountains with her dog, Stryder, a.k.a. Prince
Aragon, Melinda hikes each morning prior to
working with her clients. It is in the silence and
stillness in the mountains where she meditates
on how best to help her clientele. She is an avid
traveler, marrying her hiking together with her
adventures in foreign lands.

# The publisher

## He who stops getting better stops being good.

This is the motto of novum publishing, and our focus is on finding new manuscripts, publishing them and offering long-term support to the authors.
Our publishing house was founded in 1997, and since then it has become THE expert for new authors and has won numerous awards.

**Our editorial team will peruse each manuscript within a few weeks free of charge and without obligation.**

You will find more information about novum publishing and our books on the internet:

www.novumpublishing.com

Ingram Content Group UK Ltd.
Milton Keynes UK
UKHW041032310323
419370UK00008B/26